The Thing

Written by Jan Burchett and Sara Vogler
Illustrated by Monique Steele

Collins

4th March

It is a night with no moon.

Forks of light can be seen.

Ted, Beth and Marcos see an odd thing in the park.

It is hidden by the fort.

5th March

"The thing had sharp horns!" Ted tells us. "It had ears as big as balloons!"

"It had silver fur and big feet!" Beth tells us.

7

Marcos tells us it had a long tail.

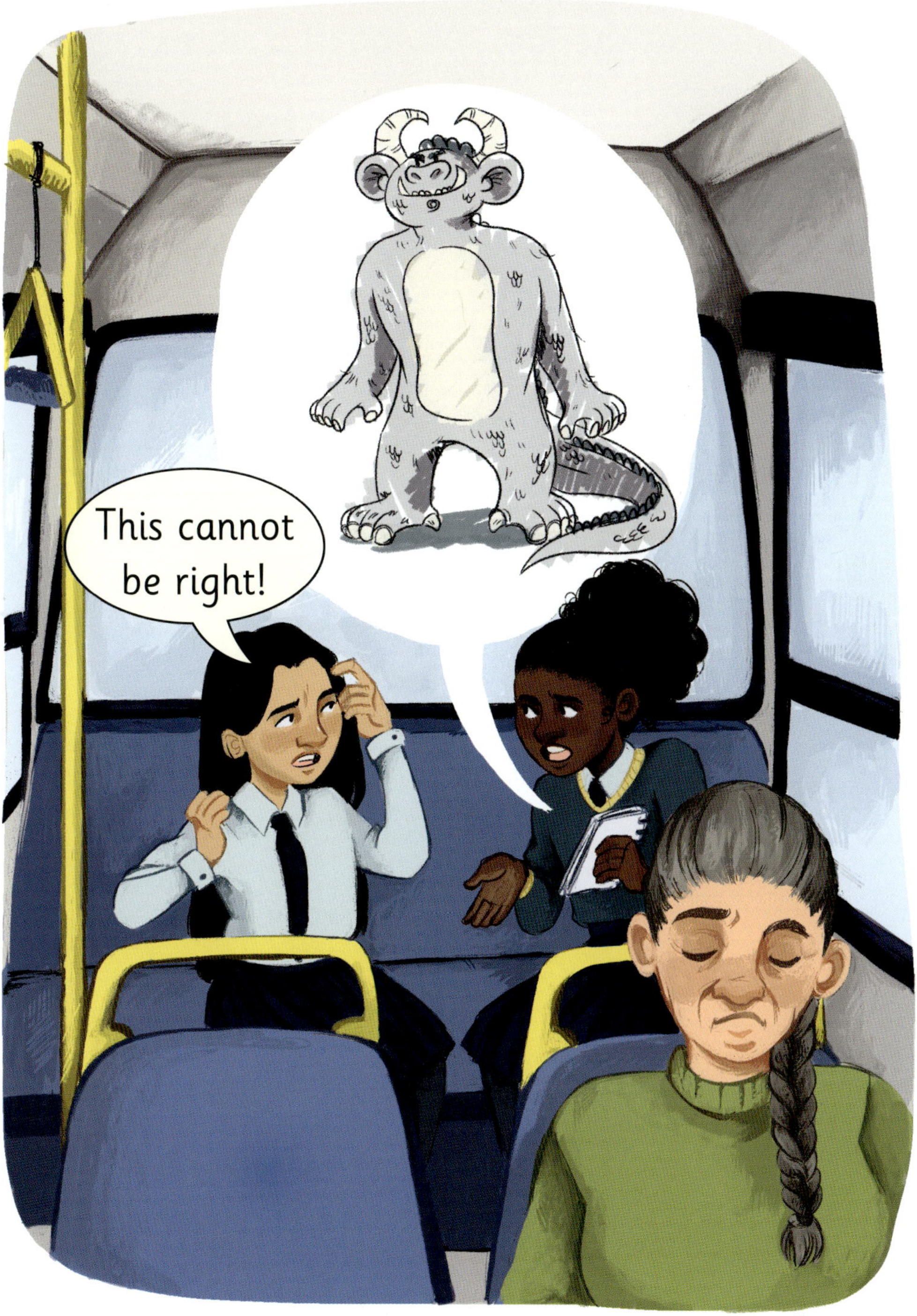
This cannot be right!

We meet at the fort. We look for horns and ears.

We look for fur and feet. We cannot see a tail.

We cannot see the odd thing.

Wait! Is this it?

Wow!

How fun!

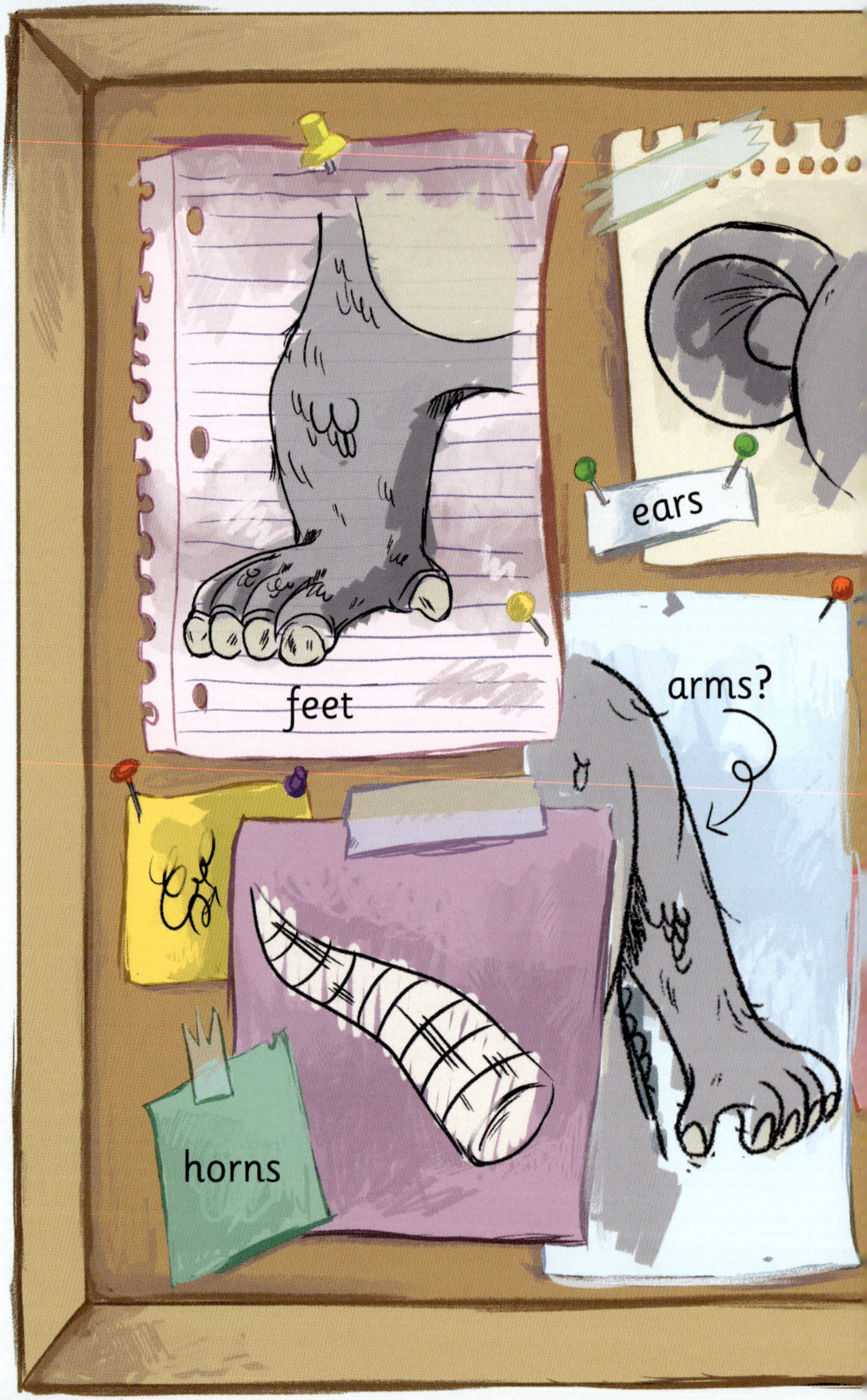
feet
ears
arms?
horns

17

Did you see this?

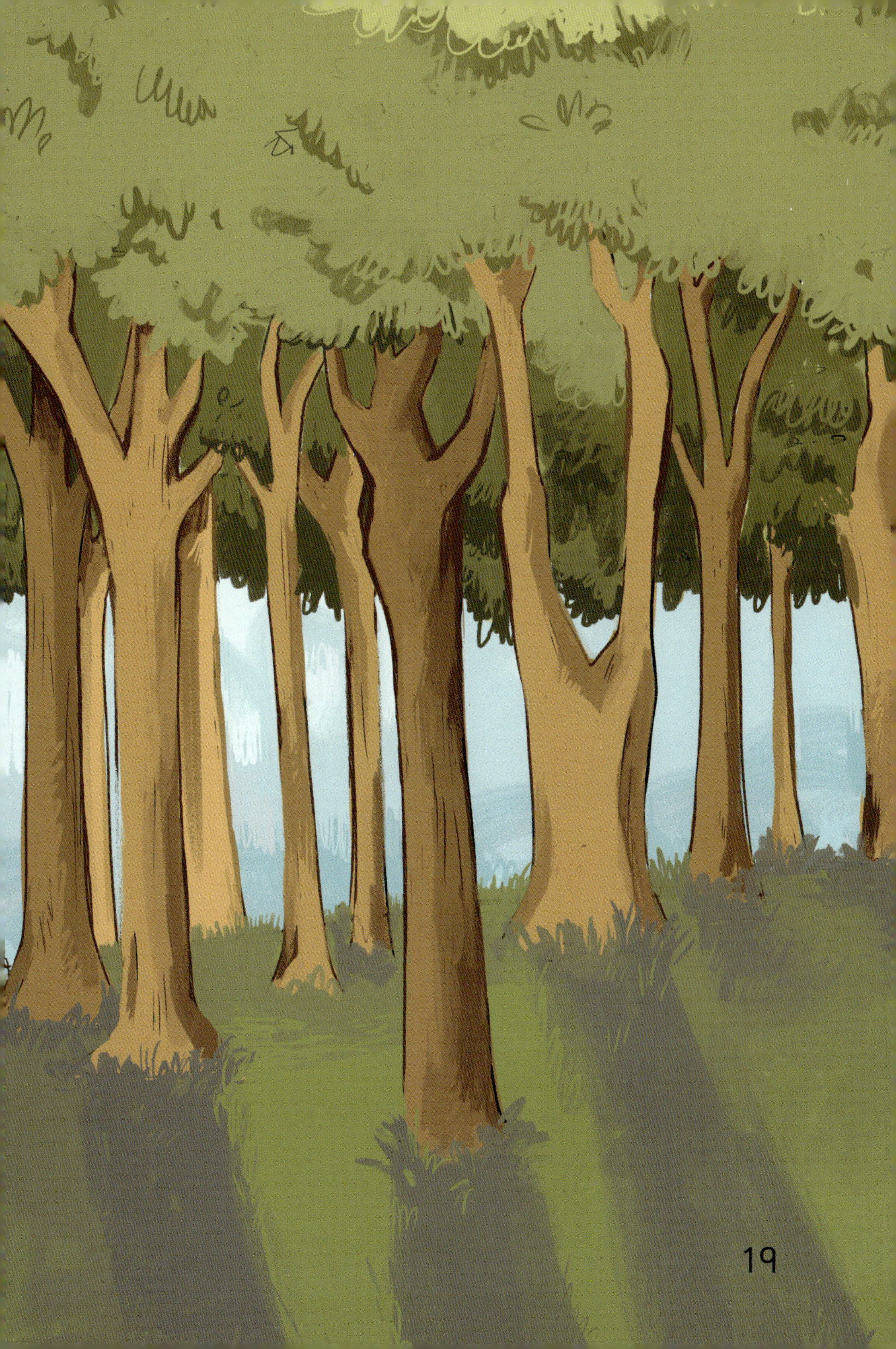

20

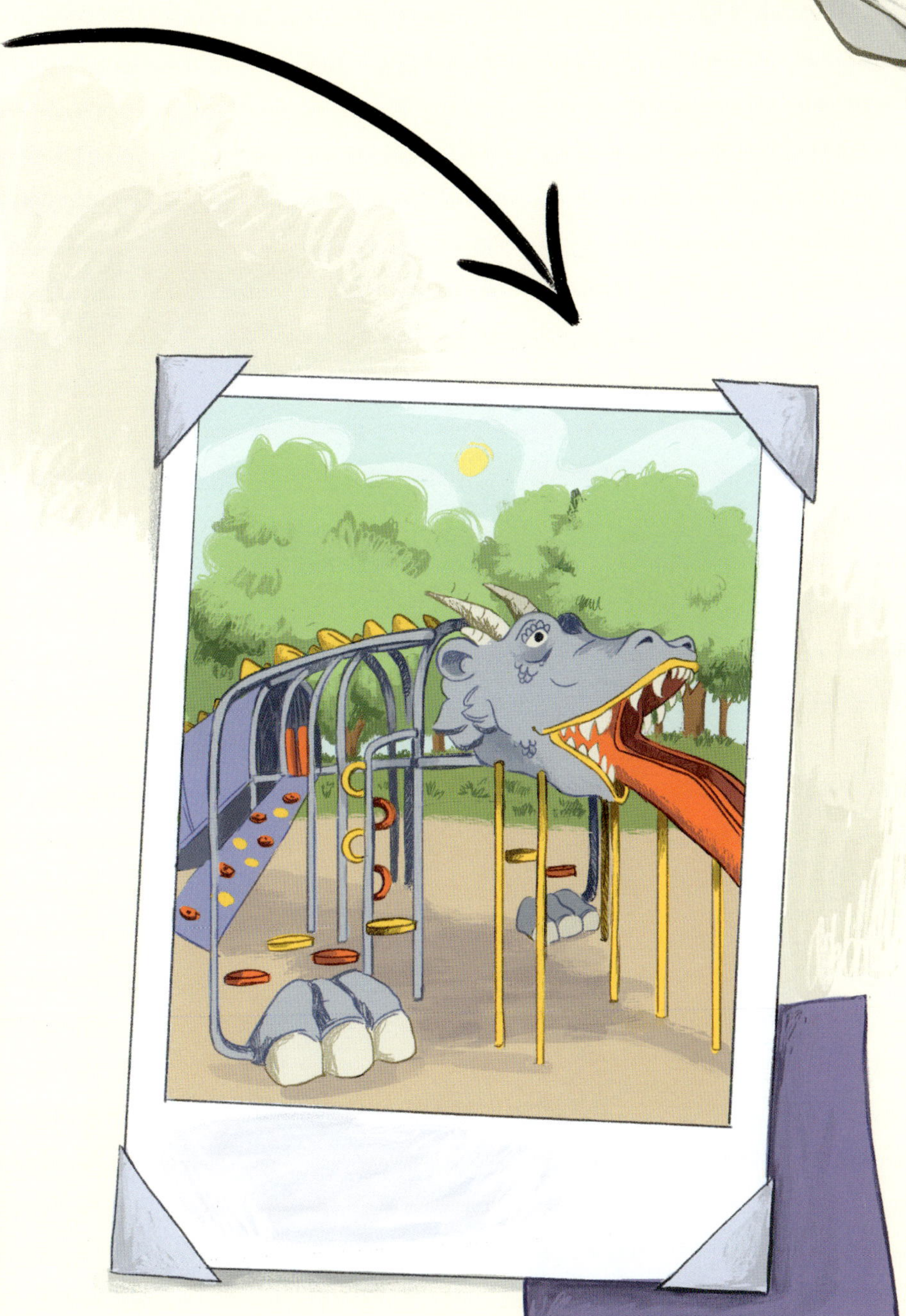

The thing

23

Review: After reading

Use your assessment from hearing the children read to choose any GPCs, words or tricky words that need additional practice.

Read 1: Decoding
- Challenge the children to read page 3. Say: Can you sound out the words in your head silently, before reading them aloud? Focus on the phrase **Forks of light**. Ask: What sort of light might this be? (*lightning*) Is it one single beam of light? (*no, it is split into parts*) Discuss how a fork you eat with is split into parts too.
- On page 6, point to **balloons** and ask the children to sound it out. Turn to page 10 and point to **look**. Ask: Does "oo" sound the same or different in this word? Encourage them to sound it out.
- Bonus content: Ask the children to read the labels on pages 16 and 17. Ask: Which two letters make one sound? (*ee, or, ai, ar, ur, th*) Which three letters make one sound? (*ear*)

Read 2: Prosody
- Turn to pages 6 and 7. Discuss how to choose a tone for Ted's and Beth's speaking voices that will match how they feel. Ask:
    - How do you think Ted is feeling? Discuss how he might want to scare or impress his friends.
    - How does Beth feel about what she has seen? Do you think she is nervous or excited, or both?
- Encourage the children to take turns to read the characters' words, showing how each character feels.

Read 3: Comprehension
- Ask the children if they have ever seen anything odd, shaped like an animal. What was it? (e.g. *a funfair ride, person dressed up, an oddly-shaped cloud or shadow*) Did it look similar to the thing in the book? In what way?
- Look together at pages 2 and 3 and discuss what makes the opening of the story scary. (e.g. *it is very dark – no moon; there is a storm*)
- Turn to pages 22 and 23 and talk about what happened in the story. Ask questions, such as:
    - What did the children think was odd about the thing? (*its sharp horns, big ears, silver fur, big feet, long tail*)
    - Were they excited or disappointed to find out what the odd thing was? Why? (e.g. *excited because they could play on it*)